ODDITIES

Who knows where the impulse to write about a particular idea comes from?
The only poem in this section attributable to a recognisable situation is
Corona does not care, the product of idleness enforced by the pandemic
Lockdown.

Autumn

Many have written an ode to Autumn,
The falling leaf, the shortening day,
The morning mist, the migrant bird
All combining to show the way
The world is walking, ever Northward,
Pointing her pole further and further away
From the left-behind sun.

The churchyard grass, still wet with dew,
The catalogue of remembered names,
The repeated promise, "…and in the morning
We will remember them."
Autumn in silence, two minutes here,
But lifetimes in the graves,
And in the still cold night
As leaves patter down leaving branches bare.

Autumn is the cold slap of air in the face
As the front door clicks behind us
The dog and I, lifted nose and ear,
To sense the distant scent and sound,
Carrying so clearly from so far.
Children at the bus stop, we share
The chill of Autumn, they in the Spring of life,
I in the Autumn of mine.

Various Verses

&

Minister's Musings

Stephen Harvey

Produced by Softwood Books, Suffolk, UK

Office 2, Wharfside House, Prentice Road, Suffolk, IP14 1RD

First Edition

Paperback ISBN: 978-1-3999-9533-7

www.softwoodbooks.com

Many modern writers feel that their poetic utterance is too restricted by the limitations of rhyme and metre to allow them to express themselves fully. While this may be true, I have boundless admiration for the classical poets of the past who frequently set themselves incredibly complex rhyming schemes and still achieved astonishingly memorable results. Almost all of the verses which follow rhyme and scan and although my structures are generally simple, I still find that the 'limitations' of pattern can actually generate unexpectedly thought-provoking results. Each to their own. I hope all of these have a certain music. Some people have enjoyed them, so I hope a wider audience may enjoy them too.

Stephen Harvey
May Cottage, Kirton
August 2024

Contents

For all who love the music of words.

We are the music makers,
And we are the dreamers of dreams

Ode by Arthur O'Shaughnessy

ST. IVES

The tightly packed houses and stony streets of St. Ives are unique. It is a beautiful place, but now with enormous numbers of visitors. Its beaches are timeless with children playing with the waves as children have since time began.

St. Ives

I look down at my tourist feet
Black the seagull shadow slides
Beneath the sun the seagull glides

I look up against the sun
White on blue in easy flight
The trailing edge a whiter white

Seaside spectrum, gold white blue
Sand, surf, sea and then the sky
Uncaught by artists though they try
The tourists go, the seagulls fly.

St. Nicholas Chapel, St. Ives

St. Nicholas Chapel on its hill-crest high,
A beacon for boats coming in from the sea.
Joining the Island onto the sky
But the door is locked—no solace for me.

"*Partially destroyed by order of the War Office.*"
So reads the notice set in the wall.
The guns of the battery watching the approaches
Needed a clear view—had to see all.

So, a chapel destroyed to facilitate fighting,
A chapel restored to the Glory of God.
Now a shut chapel is what I am writing.
For the faithful of this place the path must seem odd.

May 2023

Looking down on St. Ives Harbour

Originally a fishing village, and in the last century an artists' colony,
St. Ives is now a tourist hot-spot. It is a charming place to stay but I
always feel a sense of guilt.

Once, perhaps, a young fishwife,
Stood here, where I now stand,
Stood at this window high above
The harbour's golden sand,
Crossed with weed-hung mooring chain
Embraced by two stone piers.
After the fleet had sailed away
And left her with her fears.

An artist with his palette stood,
Perhaps, where I now stand
Stood at this window high above
The harbour's golden sand
Trying to catch, through eye and brush
The things few people see,
The shadow gull, the lifting wave,
The space where land meets sea.

Have I the right, without a care,
To sit here, drink in hand?
Sit in this window, high above

The harbour's golden sand?
I never saw a shipmate drown,
I have no Cornish past
Nor built a house of granite stone
To fight the winter blast.

June 2024

The other side

It must be about four hundred miles
West, as far as the road will go.
Through the grasslands, over the downs,
All the way down to England's toe.

St. Ives, by rights a fishermen's town,
With a harbour, church and houses of stone,
All cheek by jowl in the cobbled streets
Where the sea gulls shriek in the early dawn.

St. Ives, where the light has a bouncing gleam
Which artists paint, but never quite catch.
The palette is gold, and white and blue.
They paint it again but cannot quite match.

But where I live on the Suffolk Coast,
The sea is grey and there's not much sand.
The sun can shine on the breaking wave…
But the colour scheme does seem rather bland.

Stand on the cliffs above St. Ives
The water's so clear you look down, and *through*
Into the kelp that waves in the tide,
Hiding strange beasts of every hue.

High on the cliff I can look down
On the backs of the birds flying over the surf
Perching at will on rock or sea,
While I in my boots am glued to the turf.

Still in England but only just
As the breakers run up with the rising tide,
Whispering words of strange sea things
And unknown lands on the other side.

June 2021

Why don't they wear coats like we did,
Duffel and belted gaberdine?

They return my 'Good Morning' which
Some grown-ups do not give,
Seeing children as alien, forgetting
Their own childhoods,
Wading joyously through Autumn leaves
In their own long-ago Springs.

COMING HOME

A cup upon a saucer.
        A comb beside a purse.
A newly opened letter
        With news that might be worse.

A chair beside a table,
A draught that blows a door,
A plant that should be watered,
        A dead leaf on the floor.

Outside there may be noises,
        Pneumatic drills and cries,
The sounds of life and conflict
        May go whirling to the skies.

But here is more than silence;
        Here is quiet you can touch.
How can there just be nothing
        Where there used to be so much?

For people who are precious
        Have a touch that turns to gold
Each cup, or comb, or trinket
        Or anything they hold.

And while you know they love you
>The gold retains its shine—
Such pleasure in the looking
>At the colour and the line!

But there would be no pleasure
>And the gold would turn to lead
If the voice that once delighted
>Were an echo in your head.

If there was no answer
>When your key turned in the door,
If there was no greeting
>When your footfall shook the floor.
If there was no laughter
>In the thick deserted air,
If she had not waited,
>If she was not there,
Your jewels would be but pebbles
>And your palace but a tomb
Where all you held most precious
>Had died within your room.

Corona does not care

The pandemic lockdown in 2020 took away all three of my retirement activities, lay Ministry, school volunteering and guiding people round the Woodbridge Tide Mill. As pensioners in rural Suffolk we were very lucky; but it was still a difficult time.

Neglected on my window sill
The name tag I can't wear.
It's not that I have had my fill
As 'Literacy Volunteer.'
But they have had to close the school…
Corona does not care.

Within the bedroom cupboard hang
The robes that I can't wear.
Where once the choirs and people sang
I tried to speak so they might hear,
But they have had to close the church….
Corona does not care.

Deserted by the river side
The Tide-mill grinds no flour.
The mill pool fills with every tide--
They cannot use that power,
For they have had to close the mill
I cannot be a guide and…

Corona does not care.

We put it all behind us.
We cannot live in fear.
This glorious Spring is wondrous,
And the bird song sweet and clear.
Perhaps mankind will learn to tread more lightly on the land.
Perhaps at last from all this pain we'll come to understand
How good can come from evil and hope will follow fear......
The only thing that's certain is—Corona does not care.

April 2020

I trod a footpath overgrown

By a footpath on the edge of Frome

I trod a footpath overgrown
With buttercups and thistles sown
And found a strange memorial stone.

I'd left my wife in conversation
Deep, with her new found relation;
New love built on old foundation.

Half hid amongst the grasses green;
For many it will remain unseen.
The stone, for them, has never been.

Yet someone thought that those who pass
Should read these words and think no loss
To pause a while upon the grass,

Pausing to read, "Love lights the sun.
Love powers the world, my world. One
Till I met Love I'd not begun."

2009

Kirton Village Green

Is this a place to just pass through,
Or is it a place you might come to?
A landmark or a destination?
A place to park or for conversation?
Is this a short cut, a place to get round,
Or a place to linger where much is found?

Fifty years have now slipped by
Since grass lay open to the sky.
Fifty years and nine tall trees
Shiver their leaves in the summer breeze.
Oak and Beech and Chestnut sweet,
Casting their shade about our feet.

Every day I hear the roar
Of motors sweeping past my door.
Do their drivers, changing gear,
Realize another world is near,
A place of peaceful beauty where
One should make time to stand and stare?

Steel wheat springs from black steel furrow
Church tower watching joy and sorrow.
Artist's and blacksmith's collaboration
Made that sign in celebration

That Kirton is found in the Domesday Book
And still is a place that is worth a look.

One tree stands out against the rest.
The Christmas Tree thinks green is best
Showing life four seasons round
While others cast their clothes to ground.
Let all come here on the shortest day
When the Christmas message bids us pray.

So don't ignore this village treasure.
But stop and rest to give full measure.
For this is Kirton's Emerald Isle
In a tarmac setting so pause awhile
Where the branches filter the setting sun
Rewarding you for your jobs well done.

August 2024

Inside a Grandfather Clock

Written for a story about a treasure hunt and a long-case clock.

Nobody knows when Time began
Nor yet when Time will end.
Time brings joy to every man
Yet Time parts many a friend.
Wait not for Time yet up, and take
A step for every second.
Let him not just pass you by
As if Life never beckoned!

Tick and Tock; and Left and Right
I march from old to new.
Tock and Tick; from Wrong to Right
Do you keep walking too.
Night and day I must keep count,
And Time is what I measure.
Waste it not till you have found
My gift, your little treasure.

So do not wait for Time to go
But start your search on Monday.
The way is clear for fast and slow
And when you face me, one day,
Look at me when Time stands still,
That Time I always measure.

Look in the silence for then you will
Be guided to the treasure.

June 2020

Man

When the frost has starched the grass
    And holds the trace of where I pass,
When the shadow of a cloud
    Slides its momentary shroud
Then I humbly breathe my fill
    And thank my God for moor and hill.

Where white waters roar beneath
    The rocks which stand like broken teeth,
Where the anger of the gale
    Fells the trees across the trail,
There I stop and mutely stand
    And know that God is near at hand.

Strange how God created life
    To live in fear and constant strife.
Do we who see the hand of power
    Paint the darkening sunset hour
Derive the same uplifted awe
    From Nature, red in tooth and claw?

Did He make the stars and earth
    Before He thought of Death and Birth?
Was it all one master plan
    To make the stars, then earth, then Man?

And then?—Suppose we were to find
That God has more ideas in mind?
Suppose—(a moment of sheer terror)
That Man was just a cosmic error.

Logic says that might be so
And yet, I hope, I think, I *know*
That when I see a father's arm
Hold his child safe from harm
There is a look within his eyes
That speaks of hills and rain-washed skies.

It says that God made many things
From forest glades to fish with wings,
From waves that break upon the shore
To silent caves and gulls that soar.
But all these things have equal worth
Both living flesh and lifeless earth.

And so I think though Man *was* meant
And he *is* part of God's intent
That clearly it must be absurd
To think of Man as God's last word.
More humbly I suggest we are
The best idea He's had so far.

June 1989

How the Moon makes a Sandwich

The Woodbridge Tide Mill, where I am a guide, is a wonderful
example of how natural energy can put food into our mouths, and has
done so here since 1170.
Imagine that I am taking you outside to look at the River Deben by
moonlight, and the mill pool, and then taking you back inside to show
you each stage of the milling process.

This is the moon, all silver bright,
Drawing the tides by day and night
Into the River Deben.

This is the pond by the riverside
That fills with water on each flood tide
Pulled by the moon, all silver bright
That draws the tides by day and night
Into the River Deben.

This is the water-wheel high and wide
Pushed by water at each low tide
That comes from the pond by the riverside
Filled with water by each flood tide
Pulled by the moon, all silver bright
That draws the tides by day and night
Into the River Deben.

These are the gears with great big teeth,

With iron teeth and wooden teeth,
Turned by the water-wheel high and wide
Pushed by water at each low tide
That comes from the pond by the riverside
Filled with water by each flood tide
Pulled by the moon, all silver bright
That draws the tides by day and night
Into the River Deben.

This is the wheat that the harvest yields
Brought to the mill from the farmers' fields,
Carried up to the roof on the sack-hoist's chain,
Then brought down to the stones again.

These are the millstones cut like a harp
In ridges and grooves both heavy and sharp
Spun by the gears with great big teeth,
With iron teeth and wooden teeth,
Turned by the water-wheel high and wide
Pushed by water at each low tide
That comes from the pond by the riverside
Filled with water by each flood tide
Pulled by the moon, all silver bright
That draws the tides by day and night
Into the River Deben.

This is the flour that the millstones make

Fine and soft for bakers to bake
Into bread and rolls and succulent cake
Ground by the millstones cut like a harp
In ridges and grooves both heavy and sharp
Spun by the gears with great big teeth,
With iron teeth and wooden teeth,
Turned by the water-wheel high and wide
Pushed by water at each low tide
That comes from the pond by the riverside
Filled with water by each flood tide
Pulled by the moon, all silver bright
That draws the tides by day and night
Into the River Deben.

This is the bread and the wonderful cake
Packed in boxes for children to take
To eat at school during mid-day break
Made with the flour that the millstones make
Fine and soft for bakers to bake
Coming out of the millstones cut like a harp
In ridges and grooves both heavy and sharp
Spun by the gears with great big teeth,
With iron teeth and wooden teeth,
Turned by the water-wheel high and wide
Pushed by water at each low tide
That comes from the pond by the riverside
Filled with water by each flood tide

Pulled by the moon, all silver bright
That draws the tides by day and night
Into the River Deben.

Year 6 Leavers July 2017/18/19

*Leaving Primary School is a challenging time for Year 6 pupils
who are anxious about leaving and excited about the future, all at the
same time. I wrote this Trimlet St. Martin , to be recited by six
children at their Leavers' Assembly for the benefit of the whole class,
and they tell me it has helped them over the year*

I'm saying 'Goodbye' to many a friend
But they're still good friends to me.
Friendship need not come to an end
Old friends we'll always be.
I'll learn new things, have new ideas
And find new mates for sure
And bring them round next Saturday
And come knocking at your front door.

*Down the river of doubts and fears
Over the sea of dreams;
I'm leaving behind the last seven years
Will life be what it seems?
I don't know quite what to expect
But I have the power to be.
Others have done it and so can I
I'll make you proud of me.*

I'm an important big Year Six.
I lead you into the Hall.

I've learnt the things you are struggling with
And you come to me when I call.
But when I stand at that new school gate
Watching tall, young women and men... ...
Of all the new things in that new school
I'm the newest thing once again.

Down the river of doubts and fears...

Growing up, growing up. I've got to grow up;
But when I've gone up it's a long way down.
As I get older I hope I get bolder
But will they respect me or call me a clown?
They all say, "Don't worry. There isn't a hurry'
Just be yourself. It'll all be fine."
I suppose that's true. I won't copy you.
I'll just be me on the path that is mine.

Down the river of doubts and fears

Literacy, numeracy, open the doors
To so many wonderful places.
Now I can learn about science and stars,
About other countries and races.
Doctor, or footballer, scientist, teacher,
What kind of work will I do?
Whatever it is I'll be one of the best,

Because I went to Trimley-- like you.

Down the river of doubts and fears...

I've learnt about Romans, Egyptians and Vikings,
Cave men and Saxons and Danes.
I've learnt to look into the mystery of history
Which scholars can learn from 'remains.'
But now I have got to start looking ahead
And the future is not very clear.
What will I find on the road I must tread?
I hope there is nothing to fear.

Down the river of doubts and fears...

Sometimes we're worried by things we don't know.
The unknown is always the worst.
We never push to the front of the queue—
Always let others go first.
But once TSM was the strange new school
And look what we've managed so far.
We climbed to the top because that is the rule
For the kind of people we are.

Down the river of doubts and fears
Over the sea of dreams;
I'm leaving behind the last seven years

Will life be what it seems?
I don't know quite what to expect
But I have the power to be.
Others have done it and so can I
I'll make you proud of me.

Stephen Harvey July 2017
Verse 4 added May 2018
Vers 3 added May 2019

Multiplication

Once there was a little drip
Which trembled on a hill.
The drip became a trickle which
Would soon become a rill.
The rill drew friends around it
Which it gathered in a stream.
The stream became a river,
The home of trout and bream.
It found a bigger river
Where yet more strength was stored,
And finding weight and power
Into the sea it poured.
Now with fearsome hunger
It swept from shore to shore,
Filling rocks and sea caves
With its almighty roar.

Once a lady's little glance
Flew across a crowd,
Telling someone's secrets
Which could not be said aloud.
The glance was caught by someone
Who turned a little red,
But also, by another man
Who wondered what it said.

The men became unhappy.
Each shared it with a friend
Who called on other people,
Their honour to defend.
And soon there were two factions
Convinced that they were right,
Waiting for the moment
When they ought to start a fight.
The fight became a battle,
Which grew into a war.
And no one could remember
What they were fighting for.

Once I said a kindly thing.
I said it to a friend.
Then I found this kindly thing
Was told, repeated, penned.
And soon it seemed this little word
Hade made a hundred glad.
And when I said a bitter thing
It made a hundred sad.
Words, immortal, do not die.
They echo in tomorrow.
Love and hatred, praise, contempt
Bring lasting joy or sorrow.
Like the drip upon the hill,
They cannot be contained;

Like the lady's careless glance
Which she had not restrained.

May 2022

Steps in Ravello

Ravello sits at the top of a hill, a thousand feet, and about a thousand stone steps, above the port of Amalfi at the bottom. Wherever you walk in Ravello your passage is marked by steps, some long and sloping, some more akin to stone stairs, all gently sloping to shed the rain.

Steps climbing up, steps clambering down,
Steps are the theme of this very old town.
Go down to Amalfi. Or up to Ravello.
Or rest in this pergola where lemons hang yellow
Steps down to the sea in an endless stone fall,
Steps up to the door in the long, white-washed wall.
Under the arch and emerge near the square.
A drink before dinner. Children are there.
An impromptu dance while the parents look on.
Stone steps or dance steps? The theme still goes on.
Out at the corners streets narrow again.
Shops like small caves, brightly lit from within.
Ceramics and cameos catch women and men,
Like moths round the lamp of a bargain—and then
Steps out to the sides where gardens are waiting,
Statues of Romans give cold, solemn greeting.
The Villa Cimbrone with cloister and tower,
Bells in the town keep calling the hour.
Stepping through streets into sunshine and shade,
Stepping through life into good times and bad.

Stepping from safety to bold new ideas,
Stepping with friends who can conquer our fears.

The Husbands' Defence

To the logical mind it is perfectly clear,
If the side-plates live there and the tea-cups live here
A pile for each must be patiently stacked
While the dishwasher's trays are carefully unpacked.

Cutlery too has its classification
Sizes and functions, all have their station.
It would be an offence to an organised brain
To see fish knives and spoons laid together to drain.

Beauty is found in so many places,
Firstly, of course, in our wives' lovely faces
But also in method and organisation,
When achievement's a triumph after due preparation.

But a woman will just take an armful of crockery
Fish slices and wine glasses, making a mockery
Of any pretence to a prior inspection,
Ensuring the task is fulfilled to perfection.

How annoying it is for the hardworking male
When the kitchen resembles a large jumble sale.
His modus operandi is better and slicker.
But his much beloved wife is really much quicker.

February 2013

The Trinity

Or The Parker Sonnet
Written on the occasion of the gift of Parker 'Sonnet' fountain pen.

The virgin page, the new-filled pen and I
Each partner needing both its other friends.
Pen writing words upon the page to lie.
Mind bearing thoughts of beginnings and all ends.
Ideas, ink and paper, an ancient Trinity
Seizing and enthralling all those with eyes to see,
That everything we do is sadly lacking
If we acknowledge not another's backing.
For are we only three? Whence came this thought
I struggle to express in rhythmic line?
Some talk of Muses, of inspiration caught,
Not my invention. A gift almost divine.
I greet with joy; give thanks with all my heart.
The virgin page is now a work of Art.

April 2021

Unexpected stay in a private hospital

I did not think to be here very long.
They said the surgeon's work was swiftly done.
But sometimes, even with a well-known song,
There can be different tunes; and one,
The less familiar one, was what I sang.

Room seventeen has now become my home,
And nurses' heels clip swiftly down the hall.
Confined to bed I'm fixed. I cannot roam
But have no doubt, not any doubt at all
Kind competence is there in *every* room.

Nurses should have time enough to give
Their hard-won training, love and special skill.
And nurses also should have time to live,
And so retain compassion and the will
To comfort fearful, wounded, hurting souls.

I know and love the NHS. But here
Is difference. To feel it I'm much blessed.
What holds the two apart? To some it's clear.
The NHS needs money to be best.

I think the Nuffield holds some other treasure,
An unseen, caring thought and depth of feeling,
Which lets their nurses give in such full measure
The greatest gift of all: the gift of healing.

November 2022

ONE LITTLE VALLEY
Or THE SLEEPER RE-PURPOSED

*Newbourne Springs is a little horse-shoe valley, enclosing a stream fed
by several springs. Geologists say that rain falling on the nearby hamlet
of Foxhall makes its way through the sand to emerge at Newbourne.
The railway sleeper boardwalk makes an enchanting entry to the valley.*

Today I sleep upon the marshy ground
Touching the earth, I hear the water creeping
From where the rain falls on some sandy mound
And so it comes for ever downward seeping
Until it meets the smooth forbidding clay
From where it springs to meet the light of day.

I used to lie out on the open fell,
With cables singing sweetly overhead,
Upon my breast the weight of chair and rail,
While at my back the ballast was my bed.
With thousands of my brothers, there I lay
One vital part that made a railway.

One day men came with hammers hard and ringing,
Knocked out the wedges, took away the rails.
Loaded us on lorries, drove us clinging
To memories of skylarks in the dales.
No more the Flying Scotsman's daily flight
No more the thuds of goods trains through the night.

How different is this task, how sweet the place!
To lie beside this gently dimpling brook
So lightly burdened now as children race
To drop their sticks beneath the bridge and look
To see who won the Pooh-sticks game today,
Watching their stick go bravely on its way.

I take them dry-shod through the marsh and reed
Across the bridges, past the hidden spring
My wooden path they now no longer need
For here they tread dry ground; the path will bring
Them twisting through the sprouting hazel trees
Until they feel the summit's gentle breeze.

They wander down the valley's farther side,
The grown-ups thinking now of food and beer.
The Fox bids welcome, front door standing wide
And most forget us, though we lie so near.
Content we lie, still spell-bound by the sound,
Of waters coming, moving underground.

October 2024

CHURCH

Having been a Lay Minister for over thirty years I have served in many church buildings and been privileged to share the thoughts and prayers of wonderful people. It saddens me that many people are actually uneasy inside a church building, and many will never know the deep peace and joy that comes from shared worship. I am incredibly blessed to have enjoyed my ministry with wonderful people in wonderful buildings, and I hope that, just occasionally, I may have shared a little insight with some of them.

Kirton Church

Nothing to note, indeed!

There is nothing to note in this church except the use of septaria in the
tower, and the 13ᵗʰ century font which is open to suspicion
Description of Kirton Church in Suffolk Churches and their
Treasures. *Munro Cautley*

"There is nothing to note in this church,
Except the use of Septaria…"
Is that all you can find in your search
Of this sacred, and much loved area?

"And the thirteenth century font
Is open," you say, "to suspicion."
But how much more do you want,
O man of too much erudition?

Have you not seen how your eye
Is drawn to the Chancel and on
To the Altar, the Cross, then the sky
Out there with the yews looking down?

Have you not opened your ears
To the sigh of the wind up above,
Telling the stories of years
Of forgiveness, discovery and love?

Have you not heard of proportion,
Of arches that perfectly fit
The space where we come for devotion
Feeding our souls where we sit?

All right, it is perfectly true.
We have few architectural features.
No chancel arch framing the view,
No mysterious poppy-head creatures.

Don't think too much on the parts
Or you may not discover the whole.
Think only of heads and of hearts
And you might be ignoring the soul.

No hammer beam angels on high
No canopied tombs in the nave,
But Munro, some people come by
And pray that the Saviour will save.

April 2024

One Summer Afternoon

I had a strange encounter.
It really was quite odd.
I met a man in Levington
And wondered, "Was that God?"

I'd ridden out from home that day,
I'd washed and oiled my bike,
Thought I'd better try it out,
Check what the gears were like.

I mean—you don't expect it.
I know we go and pray,
And listen to the ancient words,
Say what we're told to say.

But you don't expect to *meet* Him,
Not really, not today,
Not when He lived three thousand miles,
Two thousand *years* away.

The afternoon was lovely,
Late summer, harvest done.
The road just led me on and on
Towards the setting sun.

And so I came to Levington,
Red tower and buttress wide,
Leaned my bike against the wall
And softly stepped inside.

I often go to Levington
But am not often able
To linger and appreciate
That lovely altar table,

With its beautiful proportions
And its glorious arching span.
I've not seen another like it---
Nor had this other man.

I'd not expected company.
I thought I'd be alone.
But there he was beside me.
Talking, this man I'd never known,

About the little pulpit
(Jacobean. Very nice.)
How the underneath pew heating
Stops your feet becoming ice.

We knelt to pray together
And I've never felt so good

Kneeling with a stranger
Midst the smell of polished wood.

"What kind of work is it you do?"
I asked in casual tones.
"Oh, I'm a carpenter." he said.
My flesh leapt on my bones.

A carpenter? The Carpenter?
It could not really be,
The Son of God from Nazareth
Just dropping in on me.

I'm still not certain who I met
Within that lovely place.
He's told us that, one day,
We will, be meeting face to face.

2019

Post Communion

May this wine and bread now broken
Be for me of Christ a token;
More than tokens let them be
Jesus Christ at work in me.

Grain once buried in the earth,
Risen tall in Spring's re-birth,
Quicken now His strength in me
Awakening who I could be.

Grape that captures sun and rain,
Holding all His power within.
Grape now transformed into wine
Let His Spirit work with mine.

May this wine and bread now broken
Be for me of Christ a token;
More than tokens let them be
Jesus Christ at work in me.

2013

Seven

There are seven instances in St. John's Gospel where he quotes Jesus saying, 'I am...' The so called 'I ams' are unique to John and remarkable because for the Jews they smacked of Jesus claiming divinity. They are also quotes that everyone remembers. "I am the Way the Truth and the Life," for example'. This poem was originally written for a ministry colleague who would instantly realise that 'four of you', in the first verse refers to the four evangelists, Matthew, Mark, Luke and John.

Strange how often the number seven
     Speaks to us of earth and heaven.
'There were four of you and three of me,
     Four men with pens and the Trinity
Seven last words I spoke from the Cross,
     Seven last words of love and loss.

And John remembered, my much loved John
     Who pondered long before writing down.
Many remembered the words they heard
     But John heard the thought giving forth the Word.
When I said, "I AM," John understood
     Seven ways in which I am God and Good.

I am the Bread and the Light and the Door.
     I am the Shepherd of rich and poor.
I am the Resurrection and the Life,

And again the Way, the Truth and the Life
Last but not least I am the Vine,
   Which carries God's strength to me and mine.'

August 2018

The Gathering

I will never be completely confident before, or after, a service. Waiting before the start I wonder who will come, if anyone, and why. And afterwards I remember all the things I missed or did not do well.

Who will come in and why do they come?
Because they ought? Or wish for some
Reassurance, a feeling of solid ground
Under faltering feet?

I wait, black robed and pale of face
Seeing friends arriving. Each week they retrace
The steps of piety, up the path.
And at the door we meet.

If they have doubts it does not show.
I may give answers. I do not know
Their needs. My words must flow
From faith—sometimes so weak!

Service over, At the door shake hands.
The pilgrims leave but…'happy bands?'
On the way to the vestry I stop. The altar.
'Father I did try.' But my words falter.

January 2023

CHRISTMAS AND EASTER

Christmas and Easter are the Church's two big festivals, telling of the birth, death and resurrection of Jesus. Over 2,000 years of teaching and speculation by the church have robbed these incredible occasions of their wonder and mystery. With hindsight we know the ends of the stories before we even start to tell them.

These three poems are the longest, and in some ways the deepest, in the collection. All three were triggered by earlier struggles in the pulpit. I try to reach back and imagine how people there at the time actually felt. Hundreds of Bishops have told us for centuries what these events signified and how they should shape our lives but how did it feel? Of course, these poems are flagrant guess-work but they felt good in the writing, and the Wine Shop in particular has been much in demand for readings at local carol services so it seems to strike a chord. I hope that they may enable a fresh look at familiar scenes.

A wine shop on the Italian shore, five years after Jesus was born

"Does anyone know what happened?"
The centurion opened his cloak,
Raised his glass with a thoughtful air,
Frowned when the other spoke.
"Nobody knows what happened, " he said,
But I tell you, you've no idea
What the world of the Jews is like
Until you've served in Judea.

"There's a boy back there." The soldier drank.
"That is if he's still alive.
I heard he'd escaped from Herod;
And my thinking is, he'll thrive.
Biding his time, I reckon,
Just growing up, learning his trade;
But one day I tell you that lad will speak
And then we'll know why we were made.

"I haven't told many people,
Not here, nor even at home.
I've followed the Emperor's eagles
Into every province of Rome.
I've always been of the Stoic school
But by all the gods above!

Surely an Emperor's officer
Follows Reason rather than Love?"

Glass in hand the officers
Over the terrace strolled.
The blood red cloaks flowed down their backs,
Before them the ocean rolled.
Away in the West the setting sun
Flashed on a hull-down sail.
In the darkened East lay a Holy Land
But they could not pierce the veil.

"The Emperor ordered a census,
(After their money, of course.)
They'd all converged on Bethlehem.
My patrols were out in force.
The inns were full, the wine flowed free
The crowds were getting quite wild
And everywhere they were whispering
Of a stable. And of a Child.

"It wasn't hard to find the place,
You just had to follow the cry
Jostling along through the alley ways
All of them shouting for joy.
But the ones you met who were coming back
They scarcely uttered a sound.

They seemed entranced, almost bemused,
They walked like men spell-bound.

"We cleared a way through the shepherd folk
But they weren't in a dangerous mood.
And the first thing I saw, when I got to the door
Was the blue of a young girl's hood.
The man looked quite a bit older,
Touched with grey in the hair.
You could smell the straw and the beasts behind......
Then I saw the Child was there.

"I realised I was kneeling,
Me! A Centurion of Rome,
There on my knees in the stable dirt
And I felt—so completely at home.
My men were kneeling behind me;
I think that we held our breath.
And each of us heard in the depths of our minds,
'Love will conquer Death.'

"Five years ago," the centurion said,
"I got a transfer home,
Cut my career short there and then
But I knew my time was come.
It's hard to make you understand
But it's what he said, you see

That helpless Child in the manger there,
Why He had come—for me!

"Nobody knows what happened,
And nobody knows what will
But I think it's coming; out of that land;
Out of the stable chill:
A completely new understanding
Of how God wants us to be
Unlocking the bonds of evil and greed
And Love, just Love is the key."

Glass in hand the officers
Stood silent, face to face
The wine-red cloaks flowed down their backs
The waters frothed like lace
Away in the West the sun had set
And the after-glow had gone.
Far in the East a child still slept....
And the officers longed for the dawn.

November 7th. 2005

Good Friday

For St. Andrews's Church Rushmere
25 March 2016

I believe I may never forget his words,
The sound of his voice, the touch of his hand.
Those three short years when he moved with us
From town to town across the land,
His was not the Pharisee talk,
Dusty words from the scrolls of the Law.
His was the wisdom of fisher folk
Hauling the net and pulling the oar.

How could he die? All hope is gone.
Darkness has come where we looked for light.
Jew and Roman have taken the Son.
The Father has shut us out in the night.

He spoke the thoughts of men who walk
In sandalled feet across the sand,
Of shepherds seeking their straying sheep,
Travellers fearing the robber band.
He could find the fish and still the storm,
Winnow the grain of the threshing floor
Jesus could always shield from harm
The unloved, the weak, the sad, the poor.

How could he die? All hope is gone
Darkness has come where we looked for light.
Jew and Roman have taken the Son.
The Father has shut us out in the night.

Remember, remember. Remember I must
His words, his prayers, his faith, his trust.
When we thought him betrayed his faith held good
While the nails bit into the flesh and wood.
So much to remember, those parables odd
Of sower and inn-keeper, master and slave
The vine and the corn-field, priest and God,
The rich who lost all and the widow who gave.

How could he die? All hope is gone.
Darkness has come where we looked for light.
Jew and Roman have taken the Son.
The Father has shut us out in the night.

So much to remember. Not long ago now
He was saying goodbye -- though we did not believe him.
Gave us the order; he'd shown us how
We should love one another—so how could we leave him?

My heart is so heavy. Now what did he say?
'Let not your heart be troubled. Ye believe in God, believe also in
me.'

But do I believe in God any more?
Shout: You let him die! Worse than that you let him be killed the
worst way possible. How can I believe either of you any more?

Forgive me, Lord. I do not mean that.
Remind me now of what you said,
In your Father's house are many rooms,
In every one a bed.
For each of us upon this earth,
You will prepare a place,
And you will come to take us there,
Our Faith received with Grace.

How can we believe? You said just look at you
And we would see the Father, the One the Good, the True.
But we have seen you done to death
By treacherous, fickle men.
Where the Father, where the Son? Where, where were you then?

Was it just last night you broke the bread,
Eyes meeting eyes as I took from your hand?
Such a taste! I have been for ever fed.
No Evil now I cannot withstand.
"Do this," you said, "to remember me,"
Breaking the Bread and pouring the Wine,
This will I do, and my children too,
For obedience as well as for memory.

How could he die? All hope is gone.
Darkness has come where we looked for light.
Jew and Roman have taken the Son.
The Father has shut us out in the night.

When the veil of the temple was torn in two
Did God fly out… or did he break in?
Help us few, to believe him and you,
That we'll meet again in spite of our sin.

January 2016

After the Crucifixion

THE DISCIPLES
It was after the Crucifixion. We were locked in the Upper Room,
Exhausted and frightened, betrayed and bereaved, awaiting the
voice of doom,
When a voice spoke gently beside us, "Peace to you all. Shalom."
And we knew from the way that he said it, that the man who had
died had come.

CHORUS
It's all about recognition. It's all about knowing He's there.
It's all about seeing Jesus in a man you may see anywhere.
It's all about seeing Jesus in the girl on the market stall,
Looking and having the eyes to see He's walking amongst us all.

MARY MAGDALENE
"I went to the tomb," said Mary, "for my heart was broken in two
And the cave was open, the body had gone. Surely sweet rest was
his due?
And I cried to the gardener, "Where has he gone? Where have they
taken my Lord?"
"Mary," He said, and I knew as He spoke that the voice was the
voice of my God.'

CHORUS
It's all about recognition. It's all about knowing He's there.

It's all about seeing Jesus in a man you may see anywhere.
It's all about seeing Jesus in the girl on the market stall,
Looking and having the eyes to see He's walking amongst us all.

TWO DISCIPLES
We were on the road to Emmaus when a man we'd not seen before
Fell in beside us, joined in our talk, and stopped at our lodging
house door.
When the bread was brought in he blessed it, broke it and vanished
from sight;
And we knew from the way that he blessed it, that we'd seen our
Lord that night.

CHORUS
It's all about recognition. It's all about knowing He's there.
It's all about seeing Jesus in a man you may see anywhere.
It's all about seeing Jesus in the girl on the market stall,
Looking and having the eyes to see He's walking amongst us all.

PETER
I took my boat to go fishing, with Nathaniel and James and John
We tried every part of the lake that night yet it seemed every fish
had gone.
Till we heard a man on the beach in the dawn cry, "Cast out the
net to the right."
And we knew by the way the fish filled the net that the Lord was
there in the light.

CHORUS

It's all about recognition. It's all about knowing He's here.
It's all about seeing Jesus in a man you may see anywhere.
It's all about seeing Jesus in the girl on the check-out till,
Looking and having the eyes to see He's walking amongst us still.

BREAKFAST

Not quite a Holy Trinity but breakfast on Saturday morning would be sadly lacking without coffee, toast and marmalade.

COFFEE

Long ago it mattered not
Whether it came from jar or pot.
Provided it was warm and brown
I took the mug and gulped it down.
But now I feel a world renewed
Each time my coffee is fresh brewed.

Is it because I have more leisure
When I indulge the simple pleasure?
Or is my taste now more attuned,
To subtlety of scent and sound?
No one sense is satisfied
Unless all five have been supplied.

First then the sound upon the tray
Of cup and saucer which I lay
With milk and sugar, nicely placed
In pattern of exquisite taste.
Thus far then I gratify
The simple wants of ear and eye.

The water hisses on the grounds.
Ah that perfection of all sounds!
With promise of the joy to feel
When that aroma starts to steal

Into the room where I shall drink
The cup of all that helps me think.

Scent has now been gratified
Still then taste remains untried.
Here Virtue Patience intervenes
And Time works magic in the beans.
Only when the time is right
I push the plunger out of sight.

All is ready! Touch the cup.
Relax before that first hot sup.
Think upon a world of love
And all good things sent from above.
Including Coffee, magic brew
To paint the world a lovelier hue.

December 2020

TOAST

Saturday, a special time
Breakfast can be long and late
The broadsheet and the marmalade
The coffee and the loaded plate

In a basket napkin lined,
Or standing in a silver rack.
Serve it as is most refined.
Then your guests will soon be back.

Straight across or cornerwise
Cut it thick or cut in thin
Not too dark we do advise
Brown outside and white within.

Marmalade

Once an Andalusian bee
      Flew to a Seville Orange tree,
Pushed its way into the flower,
      Buzzed away to another bower.
Soon the blossom petals fell.
      Soon the fruit began to swell.

Now in my hand I hold a jar.
      This bitter sweet has travelled far,
Orange and lemon securely bound
      With sugar which a farmer found
Locked in the beet of a Suffolk field.
      Now all three in the jar are sealed.

I'd like to tell that buzzing bee
      The wonderful thing she does for me,
Her sisters too in the lemon groves,
      Her cousin who over the beet field moves;
For sad it will be when the humming stops
      And there is an end of our treasured crops.

A long time past some woman or man,
      Stirring fruit in a copper pan,
With water, sugar and great invention,
      Made marmalade sweet without intention.

Perhaps their names can be found in a book...
But without the bee there will be no cook.

April 2021

Acknowledgements

This book would never have appeared without:

Susie Keepin at Woodbridge Books, the first completely disinterested professional to encourage me, Maddy Glenn, Nathan James and Jasmine Higgins at Softwood Books, for their encouragement and expertise, Abi Harold for her sensitive illustration, Jenny Fontana and Karen Cade for enabling the Kirton Writers' Group, Mark Harvey, my brother, who taught me to become much more self-critical, Alice and William, finding time in their busy lives to read and encourage, And Susan, my wife and eagle-eyed proof reader for her support which I do not acknowledge often enough.

About the Author

Stephen Harvey was born in 1947 and spent his formative years reading old fashioned fiction and poetry, a happy time but not leading to huge financial success. In spite of this he married Susan in 1977 and they have three wonderful children. He worked in the shipping industry and for Her Majesty's Customs and Excise, always feeling rather a fish out of water. In 1992 he was licensed as a Lay Reader in the Church of England which gave him an outlet for creative and spiritual thinking. (*The Gathering*) In 2008 he retired and became a volunteer at Trimley St. Martin Primary School where he found true job satisfaction for the first time. (*Year 6 Leavers' Poem.*) Sixteen years later he is still there teaching Year 6s about traditional poetry which he encourages them to learn by heart and recite. Around 2015 he became an occasional guide at the Woodbridge Tide Mill. (*How the Moon Makes a Sandwich.*)

In 2020 his three retirement activities of Church, School and Tide Mill were halted by the lockdown. (*Corona does not care.*) but like many others he turned to writing short stories and verse. If *Various Verses and Minister's Musings* finds a market, he hopes the stories may soon appear as well.

Milton Keynes UK
Ingram Content Group UK Ltd.
UKHW041444071224
452103UK00005B/346